Bamboo Shoots

My kind of poems - 400+

Philip Chan Tang Kwan

Author:

A Tale of Two Diseases

Cancer Recurrence Prevention

On January 1, 2023, I wrote my first poem.

A poem a day, every day, every syllable matters.

Bamboo shoots is a collection of "My kind of poems"

Short, simple, candid, whimsical, original,

observational, meaningful.

The audacity to write without fear of judgment.

Cover design by Philip Chan Tang Kwan.

I would like to dedicate this book
to my beautiful wife
Denise How Kin Sang.
By my side
in my heart and in my soul.

In loving memory of my parents

Mum

Teresa Lam Shang Leen

Dad

Francis Chan Tang Kwan

Fondly remembered.

Truly loved.

My thanks to Mr. Gerard Nadal

English teacher

Bhujoharry College

Port Louis

Mauritius

You instilled in me the joy of writing.

My first article was published in 1967 in the

Chinese Students' Association newsletter

"Bamboo shoots".

Port Louis – Mauritius.

My kind of poems

Cherry blossoms.

Memories of old.

Coming to the fore.

***

The mountain.

Half in sunshine.

Half in shade.

Did I come late?

***

I came.

I saw.

She conquered.

***

The Milky Way has its stars.

Jupiter, Saturn have moons.

I have you, my magic moon.

Sun rises – is this the beginning?

Sun sets – is this the end?

Both are beautiful, beginning to end.

***

She left me for another.
Often wonder
If I could have done better.
***

We looked deep
Into each other's eyes.
There were no lies.
***

Behave like a worm.
Happy to be a doormat.
Don't complain if you're stepped on.
***

Palmistry

Fate
Etched in our palms
Not in our stars.

<u>The Monarch</u>
Born in spring.
Die in the fall.
Time to make love.
No time for war.
***

Eat well. Sleep well. Exercise.
Non-smoker. Tee-total.
I saved a life. Mine.
***

When we hug
Welded together
Two hearts murmur
Sweet nothings to each other.
***

What we had was perfect.
Ended too soon.
***

China night. Shimmering candle lights.
Red and Gold floating lanterns, twinkling stars.
Dancing moonlight kept the flowering Orchids
amused.

No country for Womankind

No voice.
No choice.
Denied education.
Screaming for attention.
No sound out. The world is deaf.
No human rights, jobs, hopes or dreams.
A black hole brimful with gloom and human despair.
We are all equal, worthy of the same dignity
and respect.

<u>Together forever</u>
Everyday
We see each other.
Never tire of the deep love
We share together.
Look out for one another.
We lose ourselves
In each other's embrace.
Long tender hugs and kisses.
We mean a lot to each other.
What we have is beyond measure.

Listen to your voice.

Decide on your choice.

You'll always be YOU.

***

Self-sufficiency

Appreciative, caring, forgiving, kind,

Honesty, loyalty, sympathy, empathy.

Keep them all. You'll never ever need any from anyone.

***

"King Canute"

The tide will continue to come. No one can stop.

Wind, solar, water are the future. The best is yet
to come.

Coal is dying, dead, soon to be buried. Canary is
set free.

AI, a bullet train with no brakes, no one can stop.

Can you stop cockerels from crowing, hens from
clucking?

***

Heavy heart

A heavy load.

Empty heart

Weighs heavier.

Bamboo tree

An evergreen tree, birthing buds on branches
Growing stronger to hang frivolous daydreams.
Fresh morning dew, pale sun rays shimmering its top.
Birds hopping, chirping amid its thousand shoots.
Gentle breeze, leaves swaying, sunlight passing
through.
Faint whispers swirling. Aspiring and awe-inspiring.
Not bending, unyielding. It stands tall, strong and
resilient.

Sliding doors moments

The train arrived on time.

Shall I hop on it or wait for the next one?

What if I had said: "No thank You" to a job offer?

What if I had not gone to meet a friend, then I wouldn't have met my wife?

What if I had not gone to my doctor the day I found a lump in my neck?

So many ifs in our lives, so many defining moments.

We all have our sliding doors stories to tell.

Hop on the train, the next may not turn up.

***

Harmonica

You blow.

You suck.

Sounds come out.

***

Eulogy

Didn't know he was such a dreadful soul.

A good morning indeed

I woke up
No one to hug.
She rose early like roses do
Laden with fresh morning dew.
We had breakfast for two in bed.
You're not to know what happened next.
Thank you darling.

***

Easter fast

Forty day fast!
Not so fast.
You may not last.

***

Saving for a rainy day

Watch out.
Cuckoo's about.
Protect your nest egg.

The frog

Squatting

Thinking

Suddenly

Leapt

On a floating leaf

Heading downstream.

***

Moment of reflection
Standing, head bowed
On poppy field in full bloom
Where thousands of braves have fallen.

***

King cobra

Sets a sting

For black mamba.

***

Life is brief. Like the gentle tide that washes away
Faded footprints made strolling on a soft sandy beach.
We are merely travelers. No one leaves a lasting legacy.

Woman in black.

In a forest of blue and yellow flags.

Standing alone with her pain and sorrows.

Sobbing, a bunch of wild daffodils to cling to.

***

The Chancellor of the Exchequer

Stick and carrot budget.

To whom? For whom?

We're not asses.

***

I DO

I DO

Marriage

As dead as a Dodo.

Ode to a Pig

Number 12 on the menu.

Fat, not fit, can't fly, roasted.

Last in a line of twelve.

Couldn't outrun the rat or the ram.

Live in a modest pigsty not too far from the sky.

Not a boar nor a bore. Playful and fun to have around.

Just a smart pig, friendly and generous.

I was born in the Year of the Pig.

<u>Her Majesty's Prison</u>
Buckingham Palace.

<u>Her Majesty's weakness</u>
Baked beans on toast.

<u>Her Majesty's pleasure</u>
Prince Philip.

Is infidelity
Common among Royalty?

Queen Mongoose
Gave
King Cobra
A love bite.

Charles-Yin
Camilla-Yang
Make a good team.

Dicing with danger

We set out in earnest. White pellets pelting in darkness. It's madness.
Wintry December, the night was dark, freezing winds blowing loud.
Steering silently through hail, snow, car coated with freezing rain.
It was really insane. Fighting ice and snow, I may never be the same.
Headlights and fog lights full on, follow closely the contours
of the road.
Eyes wide, neck stretched, cool and calm, snow tires surefooted.
To spend Xmas by the Niagara Falls. It took a while. It was
worthwhile.
Dawn came. Darkness lightened. Stars disappeared. Clouds in view.
Road, quiet, deserted. Winter white. Birds dare not fly, stayed indoors.
We were brave souls, covered the treacherous miles with winning
Smiles. A December day my Missus and I will remember forever.

Bees find
Honey attractive.

***

<u>Make yourself at home</u>
Undertaker found
Napping in a made-to-measure coffin.

***

<u>Park bench</u>
Pigeons begging
Beggar's sandwich.
Nothing in between.

***

<u>Trafalgar Square</u>
Pigeon dropped a clanger
On unsuspecting Lord Nelson.

***

Ed
Going soft
In his old age.

Don't go to church.
Go to nature instead.
Never preaches.
Always teaches.

***

Poems
Allow you to imagine.
Give you wings to perch
On trees and sing songs of praise.

***

<u>David and Goliath</u>
The moth
Has landed
On a behemoth.

***

Tailor
Said to me.
"Suit yourself"

<u>Rumble in the jungle</u>
Fiesta time for meat lovers.
Oh! I could eat a zebra.
KFZzzzz.
***

<u>What a wonderful world!</u>
Pink Panther met White Elephant
On a zebra crossing.
Friends shaking hands.
Hello, how do you do?
***

<u>Table manners, kids!</u>
Lioness:
Don't play with your food.
Cubs playing with Bambi.
***

Gap between two trees, two mountains.
It's nature's winding path. Zig-zag, snakelike.
Wild, beautiful, untrodden. Virgin territory. Inspiring.

Send in the tanks. Aim them at trenches.
Park them on the blood-soaked lawn.
Turrets smoking, from dusk to dawn.
Fear to tread, mines blowing.
Shell after shell.
It's hell.

***

Why
Did I live the life I did
Now that it's too late to undo it?

***

First snowflake.
Billions more.
Winter is here.

***

Polar bear:
In Antarctica
I'd be Emperor.
In the Arctic I'm a scavenger.

When life's work done
Will there be an afterglow?
Will we ever know?
Just an afterthought.
***

Snail made it to the summit.
Boulder came crashing down.
Progress can be painfully slow.
Failure can be such a spectacle.
***

Hidden from view
Daffodils grow.
Bears snore
Under the snow.
***

In love
I learned
To keep some for myself.

Where have all the flowers gone?
Can they grow in the middle of a battlefield?

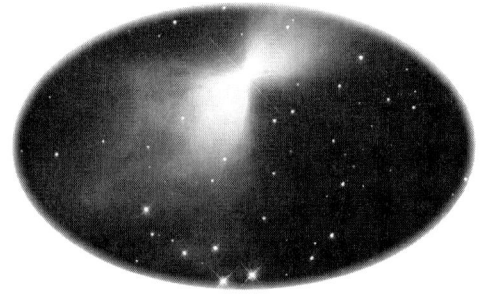

<u>Oscar night</u>
A constellation of stars.
Dimmed, underdressed, overrated.
Old hands, new faces.
Faded flowers.
Starry-eyed.

Water flows downstream.

It's gravity.

Salmon swims upstream.

It's homesickness.

***

Places to die for

Heaven overrated.

Hell understated.

Purgatory invented.

***

Am I brave?

Will I save?

My own skin or that of kin?

***

Love

Nibbles

Sucks

Bites

Deeds at speed.

Dream has wings
To fly above all things.
Soars like a kite on a string.
***

Life is short
Blooms in spring
Grows in summer
Withers in autumn
Dies in winter.
***

How far can a flat tire go?
How fast can a square wheel go?
Unless you change, you'll get nowhere fast.
***

Two lovers
Understood love in different ways
Soon parted ways.
***

She was in two minds.
Me or him?
I left.

She said:

I love you less.

I understood what she meant.

***

Do you love me?

Having to ask suggests doubt.

Having to ask twice, there's no doubt.

It's over.

***

We had to let it go.

The love dots did not connect.

It was for the best.

***

Best if we part was a good start.

The journey's lifelong.

We won't last.

***

I cared.

It was one way

All the way.

Taxation rules

By the rich

For the rich.

Rich get richer.

The poor don't pay taxes.

What a [tax] relief.

***

Sweat, blood and tears

Sloshing down the drains

Of abattoirs from morn till night.

***

A grain of sand

To fill an ocean.

A grain of rice

To fill an empty stomach.

A grain of truth

No one wants to hear.

***

Moon overslept

In cotton field.

Peace pipe
Withered olive branch
Strapped onto an ICBM
Locked on a general hospital.

***

Calm before the storm.
Calm after the storm.
Calm always returns.

***

The sound of horrors
Bombs explode. Children crying.
Women wailing. Sirens howling.
Dogs barking. Bodies silent.

***

Earthworms worn out
Deaf from battle sounds
Draining blood-soaked grounds
Dare not resurface.

Eye 2 Eye
Man 2 Man
Bayonet in hand.
Wild Wisterias witness
The horrors stayed mute.

***

Cuckoo in tears.
Laid its egg in an eagle's nest.

***

Drones raining down, monsoon season.
Soldiers in fetal position die in fear with flies.
Flame throwers scorched the trenches like incinera-
tors.
Those souls ain't going back home to rejoin loved
ones.

***

Yesterdays
Todays
Tomorrows
Jam jar
Always full of
Empty promises and fruits.

One life.

One purpose. One goal.

Is it too much to ask?

***

The sun will rise.

Not knowing whether sky

Cloudy or clear, clammy or stormy.

It will rise to face uncertainties, like humans do.

***

The sea water red with tuna blood.

A sushi bar nearby.

Sake on tap.

***

Spend

Spend

Barrowful of sorrows.

***

Peach blossoms

Sweet scents faded too soon.

Blade of grass
Green and tall.
Time to mow.
Its time has come.
***

Two long lost friends
Bumped into each other.
Had a good chinwag
Love to mate again.
***

<u>Stimulation</u>
Finger on the trigger.
Sighs of pleasure.
Climax at leisure.
***

<u>Heartless</u>
Transplant
Gone wrong.

Zodiac signs
Born a Capricorn.
Stubborn as a Ram.
Overcame canny Cancer.
Became as strong as Taurus.

***

In the wild
No fat zebras. Lean hungry lions.
No slow gazelles. Fast running cheetahs.
No poor sighted leopards. Death by starvation.
No crippled buffaloes. Pack of laughing hyenas.
No churchyard. No graveyard. No crematorium.

<u>Like a log.</u>
Floating Nile crocodile
Eyes of a periscope
Ferrying an egret
Down river.
***

Wildebeest crossing.
Crocs waiting.
Showtime wrestling.
No fun watching.
***

Forgive and forget don't work.
Indifference might.
Total indifference works well.
Why not try? Who will cry?
***

Love ended.
Head let it go.
Heart treasures it.

<u>Merry month of May</u>
Pretty nightingales
Sweet rose-breasted grosbeak
Sweeping over fields, zipping over rooftops
Gatherings insects, incubating eggs
No hazy lazy days, hungry mouths to feed.
***

Planets
Dance round the sun.
Humans
Run in circles
Round Stonehenge.
***

<u>Eerie</u>
Sound of hysterical hyenas
Young and old, at the dinner table
With their smartphones on.
***

Rain falls.
Dry grass weeps.
Accepts the gift of life.

Cancer makes no distinction
Between young and old.
Strong or weak. Takes no prisoners.
***

There are problems.
There are solutions too.
Do not despair.
The two are an inseparable pair.
***

It's a fact.
We do not chase fads.
Nor do we get seduced by hypes.
We are not those types.
***

With my motivation
Comes an explanation.
No pain, no gain.
Each day I have a goal.
It's set in gold.

<u>Family</u>
The longest
Six-letter word in history.
Before BC to AD.
***

Sugar candy
Meets Cancer.
Love at first bite.
***

A mousetrap
Smells a rat.
***

An Ostrich named
FOFO.
***

<u>Egg-dentification</u>
Spring's here.
Chickadee beware.
Cuckoo's eggs.
Powder kegs.

The Monarch
Has landed on
Lion king's nose.
***

If people avoid you
You avoid them.
***

<u>I spy</u>
Red Dragon
Ruffling
Bald Eagle's feathers
With white balloon
High in the sky.

You did it too.
Remember The U2!

God bless you two

You're beautiful. You're faithful.
A perfect pair. We are your heirs.

You care. You share.
With love, you gave your all.

I love you two.
I know you love me too. That's true.

You allow us to grow without a single row.
You let us roam, work and play.

You dried my tears, soothed my fears
Taught me to be me.

Lots of love you share
With all eleven of us under your loving care.

That boy---

Had no money.

Can't buy a lot.

Not complaining.

No new schoolbooks.

Old borrowed ones to look.

Old covers, torn pages.

Worn out shoes.

Worn out soles.

Cardboard to plug the holes.

Not a fussy eater.

Stomach never full either.

Slept on the wooden floor.

Not far from the door.

No radio, no fridge.

Outdoor life is fun.

Don't feel sorry about this story.

No two pennies to rub. As happy as sandboy.

That poor boy was me.

<u>Old friends far away</u>
The sound of waves
'Cross the wild blue waters
Carry my soft melancholic calls.
Where are you now?
How have you been?
The giant wide-winged Albatross
Crisscrossing the five oceans
Swaying lazily with
The warm air streams
Sowing seeds of friendship
New and old
I love you all.

Birds of Paradise
In far flung corners
Of the Earth
In their best attire
Celebrating Friendship Day.

Whales wave their tail fan.
Dolphins always wearing a smile
Jump and leap with joy.
Sailfish shoots to the stars
To say hello
How do you do?
We'll meet again
Somewhere, somehow.

Butterflies exhausting migration
Gather at a jamboree
Greeting each other
Wings flapping
Effects amazing.
We'll be together
Be friends forever.
Nothing can change our beautiful short life.

Rustproof

Old friends like old pots are tried and tested.

Talk non-stop. Lending hands, lending ears.

Unconditional, undemanding, forgiving.

Always on standby.

***

Cultural difference

East meets West.

The two shall bind, feet and breast.

Lotus shoes with matching Lotus bras.

***

Be realistic

It's unlikely for Derek the donkey winning the derby.

Or Helena the hyena "au naturel" winning Miss World.

Or Harry the humpback winning over Molly the Mermaid!

The World a stage

Actor, Demonstrator, Innovator
Conspirator, Doctor, Author.
Are you a tailor, sailor
Or just plain Elizabeth Taylor?

***

Spring roll

Smiling green toad
Rolled out its sticky tongue
Like a welcome rug.
Rolled in its prey still smiling.

***

Is there ever a good time to look back
When there's so much to look forward to?
Better shape the future than singing about the past.

***

Moonlight. Ocean bright. Mirror-like.
Apart, we see, share the same moon and stars.
Like the Adonis blue, I'll fly through monsoons, lightning
To be with you, be near you on super harvest moon
night.

Solo sailor and the sea

Sailing the seven seas
Horizon beckons.
No breeze.
Cruel winds.
Calm waters.
Savage seas.
Hopes high and low.
On your own.
Still whole.
You're going home.
The sea still beckons.

Jumping off
London Tower Bridge is OK
Until you hit the River Thames' water.

**

Conflict over.
Roads cleared.
Corpses on wagons pass.

**

On killing fields
A lone drummer boy
Stood tears in his eyes. Drum beats.
No one left to march. Standard bearer MIA.
Mists and fog, branches bow, heavy with mourning dew.

Two golden eagles
High–fives
In the sky.
Talons out.
No feather ruffled.

***

In retirement
Thumb twiddling.
Stomach rumbling.
Waist expanding.

***

Obesity
Eating
Has nothing to do
With hunger.

***

Tax deadline
Professional beggar
Filed tax return on time.

That's not light
At the end of the tunnel.
It's burning orange bright.

***

<u>Heavy lifting</u>
Atlas carries human burdens.
Ended up in ER with a hernia.

<u>Antique roadshow</u>
At 92, on concert tour
A farewell "tour" many.

***

Rain falling.
Together we go
Down the drain.

Bees in tears
As they leave
The Peonies.

***

Stick with it.
Never give up.
Try eating custard
With chopsticks!!

***

<u>Black swan day</u>
Fat happy chunky turkey
Fed daily with TLC
Did not see it coming.
Thanksgiving Day.

***

Open neck blouse.
Firefly gatecrash.

***

Fuchsia flowers fell.
I left with regrets.

Canada Revenue Agency

It doesn't add up.

Call the

"Adder"

***

Squirrel stocktaking.

One acorn missing.

Auditor called in.

***

The 1st of Spring

River thaws.

Fish emerge.

Bears reappear.

***

Arrival and departure

On a chilly wintry day

On the first floor

A newborn baby arrived.

On the third floor

An old codger departed.

Beauty of time

Ever since time begun

Raindrops

Drop by drop

Turned canals

Into canyons.

Hooked to an IV

Tick, tick, tick.

Drip, drip, drip.

Chemo drugs on a trip

Seeking tumors with license to kill.

***

Snowdrops and daffodils

Taller than the melting snow

Emerged from ground zero.

***

Female birds

Don't sing when incubating.

They keep their wings crossed.

Wrote this Ode
To celebrate a successful
Non-Hodgkin Lymphoma cancer treatment.

Ode to health

Hair shining and light
Eyes sparkling and bright
Nose knows it's alright
Tongue pink, gums tight.
Hands and arms steady
Skin glows, liver healthy
Bone and marrow hardy
Body lean and hungry
Head, temples, neck
Ear, nose and throat
Shoulder, head, abdomen
No aches, no pain
Healthy State.
No cancer.

Mayday, Mayday.
There's a Cuckoo
In my nest.

***

Seashells
On the shore
Wet with rain.

***

Hot summer.
Cold sweats.
Meeting in-laws.

Donkey
Stubborn
Calmness.
***

Beaver dives.
Home dry.
***

Beggar
Paper cup in hand.
Beggar's child
Birthday balloon in hand
Looks wearily
At passers-by.
***

<u>Men's game</u>
Let's see
Which side
Got more balls.

<u>Rome was rebuilt</u>
Bombs shatter buildings
Not human spirits.
Vietnam is thriving.
Ukraine will rise
From the ashes.

Dog saw a shadow.

It barks.

Other dogs heard the sound.

They all start barking mad.

***

It's all fun and games

Snakes and ladders.

Rollercoasters.

Life's a roll of dice.

***

Turf war

Chalk lines.

White powder.

Clear divide.

Sniff, snort.

Up the snouts.

Head blown off.

***

Immune system

Bull in a china shop.

<u>Mane attraction</u>

They have pride.

Those without

Have room to roam elsewhere.

She is best mate

To one or more males.

She rears and cares

Hunts and feeds the cubs.

Daddy is a security guard.

Dozy, lazy, slumbers like a lamb.

With a mighty roar

He rose, towering high

His Majesty surveying

His pride with great pride.

***

<u>Dream big</u>

Baboon dreaming

2B

King Kong.

<u>Ode to the golden bat</u>
A fly by night
Upside down view of the world.
Loved by bananas, enjoys a few dates too.

A hanger on
With moon for a clock
Night for a cloak.

Silent as a submarine
Beeping and clicking
When night hunting.

I'm a Rodrigues flying fox.
Sociable, hang out with cousins
From Mauritius and Madagascar.

Endangered.
Only a few of us left.
In the Black River Gorges Park.

Salmon
And
Ella
A deadly duo.

***

<u>Life in seconds</u>
<u>b</u>
<u>d</u>
<u>r.i.p</u>

Live lobster
Stared at me.
I put the knife down.

***

Midnight.
The clock strikes 12.
Night becomes day.

***

<u>Progress</u>
One step forward
Two steps back
Two forward
One back.

***

<u>The Royals</u>
Kate – Kittenish
Harry – A Spare
William – The conqueror
Meaghan has Harry as a Spare.

A seafarer

I sail the seas.
The stars above
Are guides and guardians.
The wind is my trusted friend.
Have pals everywhere.
Polars in the North
Emperors in the South
Mermaids in every port.
Swallows fly past.
Cheers as I sail in.
Tears as I sail out.
On the crest of a wave.

Gorilla

Beating about

In the bush.

***

<u>Montreal Zoo</u>

Plenty of

Zoo-Loos.

***

<u>Wet Wet Wet</u>

Wet weather.

Wet snow.

Wet dream.

***

Chick

With longer neck gets more food.

***

<u>Our history</u>

Not twisted, never unkind.

Loving and respected.

We parted. It was fated.

Endangered.
Adopt me.

<u>The Dow Index</u>
Dow rises like a soufflé.
Falls like a flat bread.
Rise or fall,
There's dough to be made.

The lady from Nantes
Ego of an elephant
Brain of an ant
Was my late Aunt.
***

Home again
Spider in the tub
I scooped it up
Back to its web.
***

Hummingbird
Hmmm
Humbling.
***

Half-moon.
Half-hearted.
Why not in full?
Could be a whole lot better.
***

Moon hanging out with stars
Has good company all night long.

She-wolf

I'm not who you think I am.

Not a She-Wolf in sheep's clothing

Even though my fur feels like sheepskin.

Proud, wild and free, I live in a pack with family.

At times, I like to be a lone wolf, with private thoughts.

On a moonlit night, you can see me up in the mountains

Down in the valleys, roaming or rolling in the fine snow

Sitting with head high, not howling, not crying wolf

Or wolf whistling at passers-by. It's so unladylike.

I'm not the big bad wolf of the fable.

As sweet as Red Riding Hood.

We could've been the best of friends.

Destination uncharted

Small boat, pair of oars
On my own, on a deserted lake.
Heading out, steady as she goes.
Tears running, leaving behind shingle beach
Tall casuarina trees and black rocks on each side.
Clear, calm, beaver moon, still silent night.
No roars, oars in hands
Row to meet with destiny.

<u>One woman and her dog</u>
Sheep and shepherdess.
Perhaps a better style of Government.
***

Giraffes
Mating
Mile high.
***

<u>Piano tuning</u>
Silence
Between
Two notes.
Deafening.
***

Ducklings
Fall one by one
Into a drain.
Plop, plop
Gone.

<u>A stunner</u>
Out of the blue
A forget-me-not
Peeped shyly through the crack
Of a deep freefall cliff.
Staring, sighing, longing
A heart-breaking reminder
Of a very beautiful girl
I once knew who was out of reach
Like the flower in the cliffside.

<u>Miss your kiss</u>
The last kiss
Was the best of them all.

Slow on the take

I misunderstood.
I didn't know what love is
And how to love you.

You gave me chances upon chances.
I was too blind to see romances.
So green. Such a loss.

I realized too late.
You left and met another
Who knows what love is and how to love you.

I won't forget you.
Wish you well.
Farewell.

On second thought

Waded into the freezing water.
It's too cold to die.
Better wait till springtime.

Spring came.
Birds are singing everywhere.
Trees are budding. Peonies are blooming.

There's no good time to die.
All the seasons are joyful and cheerful.
Four reasons to live a day longer.

Independence Day

I'll cling on your tailcoat
Till the gales died down
Till the floods subsided.
I'll then be on my way
To some place far away
To learn to be on my own
To pick myself up when down
To return a man.

No coin is one-sided.
Two-faced?
Maybe?

***

My sweetheart
Risk averse
Married me.

***

Like the sun
I can be hot.
Like the moon
I can be cool.
Like Earth
I'm beautiful.

***

Winter losing its bite. Lost its cool.
Less white. Autumn golden mellow brown.
Climate crisis, winter may wither, shrivel and die.
One season less, who will miss it? Who may care?
No snow-capped mountains, snowman, or Snow White.

<u>Waves of comfort</u>

Dancing with the waves
Soothes my pain, allays my fears
Dispels my worries.
We meet on Blue Bay Beach
Like the sky meets the horizon.
The sea looks perfect.
The mighty ocean waves
From the Pacific to the Atlantic
Meeting the Indian halfway.
Submerge my fresh footprints
On the white sanded beach
Washing away my worries.

<u>Panda in love</u>

Ding Ding

rings

Ding Dong.

She's been waiting too long.

Ding Ding

loves

Ding Dong.

They have a beautiful daughter

Cha Cha

who loves to Cha Cha Cha.

***

<u>Cherry blossoms Sakura season</u>

Seven blossoming days

Make a blooming week.

They wither and fall in splendor.

The flowers will reincarnate.

More vibrant, fragrant and elegant.

Admirers will enjoy your scented shade again.

<u>Kama Sutra</u>
Number 69
Breathe. Relax.
Enjoy. Imagine
Yin and Yang symbol.
Harmony and Balance.
Go for 79
Bingo!
One more time
Baby
One more time
For old times' sake.

A houseplant
Does not get to know
How cold it can be outside.
***

Cancer
Make sure
It does not have
A return ticket.
***

Lady in Prada
Wolf-whistles
Bob the builder.
***

The old mirror looks the same.
My reflections are not.
But they look happy just the same.
***

A dog
Is not God.
Some Docs think they are.

Caterpillars
Become butterflies.
Parents
Become Grandparents
Overnight.

***

Wet kiss
Under the rainbow.

***

Caesar salad
He was a Roman.
Sirloin.
He was Henry VIII.

Rich kid, Poor kid

Poverty

Was never a handicap.

We travelled

The same mountain road.

Climb the same hills and trees.

Swim in the same sea.

Laugh at the same old jokes.

Play truant together.

He has pocket money.

I have none.

That was never a handicap.

We looked

At the same sky and stars

Lit up by the same moonlight.

Share sunrise and sunset stories.

But a girlfriend is not for sharing.

We are best friends.

A poor kid and a rich kid.

<u>Spring offensive</u>
Daffodils in bloom.
Nature greening.
Bees buzzing.
Nation fights nation.

Flowers die in birth.
No plaintive cry heard.
Soldiers succumbed without firing a shot.
Tanks crushing new budding grass.

Winter of discontent.
Drone grenades raining down.
Trenches in flames.
The season of goodwill getting hell hot!

They labored six foot deep in zigzag trenches.
Digging graves for themselves and for fellow comrades.
They're noughts with crosses above.
Wishing it was only a game.

They're going home in bags, coffins or urns.
Ashes on the ground, scattered by the breeze.
They are resting. It's their new hometown.

Have you heard the sound
Of lamenting bagpipes and drums?
No one listening, they're all screaming.

Leaders, Generals plotting.
Grave diggers digging.
Crematoriums smoking.

Poppies remained red.
Well irrigated by blood.
Growing and blooming
On Remembrance Day.

Old bird
Does not sing.

***

Why mimic
When
UR unique?

***

A lame horse
Is a dead horse.

***

Even dreams
Have deadlines.

***

I'm strong.
That's good enough.
I'm brave.
No need to be a hero.
Happy to keep the status quo.

<u>Loving you</u>
The first love
She thought was the best
Until they parted.
The second love
Became the next best.
Fifty years on
She's still with second best.

If you call, I'll follow the echo
Across the waters. the deserts
To be near you, to be with you.
Just whisper and I'll be there.
***

Forgive!!
Forget it.
Not going to happen.
***

Sardine calling a sprat, a prat.
Squid calling jellyfish, brainless, Starfish headless.
Owl with roving eyes given a warning.
***

Don't kneel, pray and wait.
Pray, get up and go
For what you've asked for.
***

Blood transfusion
There may be bad blood
Amongst the blue bloods.

Spare Harry
Spoil Meaghan
That's noble.
***

Sonar sound
The enemy above.
The enemy below.
A game of stop and go.
Ping, ping, ping.
Boom, bang, bang.
The end.
***

Is there not
A cool spot
Even in hell?
***

The scarecrow remained unbowed
Even as new King Charles III passed by
In his golden chariot, pulled by eight white horses.
Hat remained on. He wore his crown. So, what's
the fuss?

Decades ago
I was thoroughly smitten
By her smiles, eyes, walk, talk, body and beauty.
We lived in the same green valley,
wildflowers everywhere.
Only a heartbeat apart, too soon
we left the island of dreams,
Dodo and rum, Garden of Eden,
to study, work and live overseas.
She lived in the South. I lived in the North.
Only 300 miles apart.
Then we both uprooted. She lives with
her darling in the West.
I live with my dearest in the East.
We know each other well.

American dream
To be the "one percenter"
Sod the rest.
Chinese dream
To be the "99 percenter"
Sod the rest.
***

Drink like a fish
Piss like a dog, foot on the wall
For dignified support.
***

Friendless
Had no doubt when I found out
No one concerned
About my whereabouts.
Abandoned even by my dog.
***

In dark times, in sad times
One bulb on a Xmas tree
Gives enough light to spark joy.

Much ado about nothing
A good for nothing
In Britain
Did nothing [Niksen]
In Sweden
Is a sweet nothing
"La dolce far niente"
In Verona.

***

Singer sings.
A thousand cheers.
Politician promises, a million believers.

***

Cardinal confession
Oops!
Poops!
Holy crap.

***

Run nun run
Bishop misbehaving.

Reel in a sardine.
It's a small fry.
Reel in a blue marlin.
Too big to fry.

***

<u>Exams paper</u>
A burning question
Was set on fire.

***

Rotten egg
Fell foul of
Egg-cellence.

***

There's an UFO
In my soup.

Light travels fast.
Lies travel faster.
Bend the truth.

***

Sweeping statement
By cleaning lady
On the floor of
The House of Commons.

***

Feel too much.
Think too much.
Rest and chill.

***

The white elephant
Is
An albino.

***

Giraffe
Caught looking down
On a Chihuahua.

<u>A female bird</u>
Ladybird
***

<u>A female butterfly</u>
Madame Butterfly.
***

<u>Snow White</u>
A man a day
Even on a Sunday.
***

Band leader
Faced the music
Baton in hand.

<u>Eastern flight</u>
On a clear Arabian night
Alibaba on his flying mat
Was floating like a bat
With the silvery moon
As his guiding light.

***

On death row
Noose round his neck
He made his last request.
Dear Mr. Postman
Here's my forwarding address.

<u>Spin Doctor</u>

Come on

Let's twist the facts again

Twisting time is here.

***

Forty-nine-inch waist

Wasteful

After dinner speaker

Mouthful

Hate preacher

Hateful

Lover

Playful.

***

Why is it so painful

To let go of stress, worries and anxieties?

***

Red snapper

Finds wriggling worm attractive.

Got hooked.

The Moon
Represents my heart.
The sun
My dispositions
Hell
My intentions.
***

I can cross the seas.
Climb over hills and peaks.
Fly to the moon and back.
I can't cross over this land of mine
It's mined!!
***

Land of the rising sun.
Moon getting thinner
Settled on the National Diet.
***

At break of dawn
Bison breathe, dry steaming
Its bearskin hat.

Shellfish
Sells seashells
On the seashore
Of the Seychelles.
***

All the perfume of Arabia
And all the tea in China
Blended together
To make a great British cuppa.
***

Knocked from behind
Stars in her eyes.
***

Lost consciousness?
Try the sub-conscious.
***

Autumn
Frosted leaves
Fell into empty nest.
Only broken shell left.

What's in the bag?
A black cat.
Open the bag.
Please don't let
The cat out of the bag.

***

Fat spilled
From the frying pan
Into the fire.

***

Arab fell asleep
On a lovely moor.
Woke up
With a heavy dew.

***

Like a teabag
I know how strong I can be.
I've been in hot water before.

***

Old sycamore tree cut.
Sun rises earlier than usual.

Heaven above.

Hell below.

Stay put

Below heaven, above hell.

You're in purgatory territory.

***

He used to cut corners.

He's more rounded now.

***

Birds can fly.

The dodo can't.

That's not good.

***

Rose blooms

That's a miracle.

I can whistle, so can my kettle.

***

High-wire act.

A dove has landed.

An eagle snatched like lightning.

Sheep calms ewe.
Parrot repeats.
Sheep calms ewe.
Sheep calms ewe.
Arrrgh!*# shut this parrot up!!

***

<u>Endangered</u>
Pray for the Osprey.

<u>Hiring</u>
One dancer short.
No tango tonight.

The elephant
In the room
Making a trunk call.

My teapot
Too hot to handle
Has a goldfish pout.

Sunflower seeds sown in spring
Alongside landmines.
Harvest of death in autumn.
Bleak mournful winter.

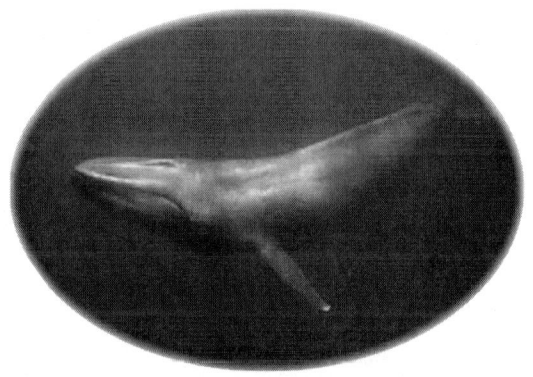

A sprat
Causing ripples
In a shallow puddle
Believed that with
The help of a few friends
They can make waves
Like a blue whale.

I enjoy Goodreads.
A bad one
I leave it to the bookworms
To finish it off.

***

Bookworm
I started
So I finished.

***

Head of State
Left on a mantelpiece
To gather dust, insult and web.

***

On death bed.
What's left unsaid?
"I love you"
Whispered so sweetly.

***

* Winter rain sticks on duck's back.
* Can he get any lower? Yes. Six feet deep.
* Sleepless night. Mosquito overstayed.

<u>King Charles III decree</u>
<u>Imperial weights & measures</u>
A pint of pink champagne.
One could comfortably drink with pleasure.
A pound of Redhill strawberries.
One could delight with ounces of Devon double cream.
The friendship with the Republic is
only 25 fathoms deep.
Brexit: English Channel parted,
21 miles and 3 yards wide.

***

Beggars
Don't
WFH.

***

Food prices
High or low
I buy the best.

What if

Your car stutters

Smoke coming off its wing mirrors.

Tires are flat.

Biscuits and vomit on the seat.

Roof leaks.

H&V system caput.

The cat shit on the carpet.

House in utter clutter.

What if

This is the state you're in?

***

Crocodile

Tears up

Over a dead gazelle.

Written in the stars

Before the cherry blossoms lose their flowers
I had packed my bag, left my bare apartment
And never looked back.

Destiny called.
I departed Glasgow for London.
Not unhappy. I was lonely.

Down south, I met a girl
As beautiful as can be.
In no time, I was on one bended knee.

It was destiny, life-changing.
With the girl of my dreams in my arms
Sayonara loneliness.

Like the Redwood tree we'll live and love
Till time grows tired and old.

Kangaroos

Have

Deep pockets.

***

Pickpocket

Got a black eye from a "roo"

***

I'm a warrior. Not a worrier.

I conquered cancer.

Without fear.

***

As a rule

I don't preach

Nor deliver sermons

Don't take confessions

Nor administer absolutions

I'm no better or worse than anyone else.

***

Hello sailor!

Sailfish wriggles its tail

All dew-eyed.

The choice you make

Cream rises effortlessly to the top.

Sediments linger heavy at the bottom.

You choose your friends

Cream or sediment

The choice is yours.

Birds of paradise don't mix with vultures.

***

We care for each other.

That's all I care about.

I've no other cares.

***

Summer sun fading. On time, autumn is here.

Never fails to arrive, dressed in gold to impress.

Summer visitors disappear on the wings, without singing.

Arctic Terns leaves, flying from pole to pole, on the quiet.

Leaves leave crestfallen. Branches, all naked feel
the chill.

Winter winds come and go, howling, nothing to blow.

Tree stood still, sturdy, not bowed nor bent. Sad and quiet.

Long silent cold nights, short days of mists and pale
lights.

<u>Distant thunder</u>
Mother in law.

<u>Distant drums</u>
Door to door salesman.
***

With mounting age, I've less rage.
With more money, less time to spend
On things not worth the time and money.
***

<u>Banns of marriage</u>
Church against it.
Parents doubted it.
Eloped to Gretna Green.
Haggis and Whisky.

The seeds of life

From seeds to forests.

Carried on the back of ocean currents.

Blown from far away by the winds.

Flown by birds to distant lands on a whim.

Enjoy the shades the seeds of life gave us in spades.

Preserve, protect them for future generations
and beyond.

A sailing boat knows too well
Its home is not in a safe harbor.
Born to sail and roam the seas.

The horizon is vast.
Sail with the wind, fair or fierce.
Ready and steady on the crest of a wave.

From pole to pole
Sailing east to west
Be back to where it all started.

Like a fish
Forever swimming in the seas
Set sail as soon as well rested.

Swarm of swallows fly past.
Sailor stopped roaming.
It's Land's End.

I'm water, fluid and soft.
Surface as hard as rock.
Winter or not.

***

What can become of
The Amazon Forest?
A Gobi Desert?

***

Manners matter.
Thank you.

***

Say the magic word
"Please"
"Open sesame"

***

The old soul
In his old shoes
Both are wearing well.

<u>In a nutshell</u>

Idolized juke boxes.
Neglected schoolbooks.
Long hair. Attention deficit.

Girls, girls, girls.
Gigi, disco and fun.
Growing up in the hippy sixties.

Worked hard and smart.
The present looks good.
Future looks better.

Be yourself.
Enjoy what you do.
Life can be simple and good.

<u>Gone with the wind</u>
Have you heard about the herd
On farting suppressant?
***

Snowflake is featherweight.
A scold, it's gone.
A whisper, it melts.
***

Turn over a new leaf.
Found a bookworm.
Took the leaf out.
***

Bucket list.
A hole in my bucket.
It went AWOL.
***

Depression! Is it mental or is it physical? Or both?
It affects not only you, but also all those who love you.
Fight it with physical activity. Fight it with mental agility.
Fight it like Churchill. Never surrender to the "black dog".

The river

The river from its source
Boldly goes, glows and flows.
Wildflowers flanked both banks.
True to its words, it never goes backwards.
Born wild and free, no worry
Rushing down mountain peaks
At speed to valleys down below
Meandering its way to the sea.
Patiently triumphs over stubborn obstacles
Carves its way through rocks and granite
Moving water is moving to watch
Powerful and graceful as it descends
A grand rapid, fascinating, foaming and mesmerizing
Follow the contours, fluid and elegant
Others smaller rivers joined in and together
They wow and vow to never return to its source.

Your love
I cannot lose
What I never had.

***

Winter long gone.
Spring soon fading.
It's June, let's adjourn
For the summer season.
Back in autumn
Rested and plump
To welcome winter once more.

***

Building Noah's Ark.
World in the dark.
Warning stark.
We are blind.
No one left behind.
Biblical floods rushed in.

Winds howling.

Door opens.

Bear cub enters.

***

Skylarks, not larking.

Dogs not barking.

Elephants seeking the heights.

Angels not harking.

Birds down their hatchers.

It's eerily odd.

The End is nigh.

***

It's uncommon

The use of commonsense.

***

Deep sea creature

A face only

A mother could love.

***

Conflicts, suffering, hunger.

Bluebells bloom regardless.

Don't feel SAD when seasons change.
There's something good in all of them.
Enjoy springtime, remember it in wintertime.
Summertime is easy, autumn is cool and calm.
***

Quid pro quo
tibi digitis dorsum
i digitis tuis
***

Pro bono
I helped the poor.
Gave generously to the disadvantaged.
Now that I'm poor
The poor are still poor and disadvantaged.
I wished that I had not been impoverished.
***

Rhino without horn lives longer.
Tunas are canned. Baby seals – clubbed.
Lucky Crow. Oversupply, not in demand.

Between U and I
Set up an UID
Declared UDI
Use IUD
Nicked for DUI
***

Feudalism
Grace and favor
Until the guillotine drops.
***

Two seagulls
Kamikaze
My fish and chips
On Brighton beach.
***

Power of word
One word from my schoolteacher:
"Praiseworthy"
I am who I am today.

Silk dress
Contours curves.
Desires awaken.

***

Leaves fall
In the fall
All crestfallen.

Forgetfulness
Not
Forgiveness
Makes for happy.

***

Humble baby
Grown in a lab, test-tube life.

***

A grain of sand in the eye
Caused a biblical flood!

Dawn breaks.
Break my fast.
Break wind.

***

A fishmonger and a fear-monger
Caused a tsunami
In seafood prices.

***

Flowers fold for the night.
Well rested and refreshed
Open up at first light, all scented
To meet and greet
Me and my friend the Red Admiral.

***

A single sand
Landed on my land
Blown from Swaziland
Still in one piece!

***

Lavender blossoms in their thousands
In soils company of heroes died unsung.

A deep well.

A frog cocoon world.

Turtle wishing it well.

Beyond, there's another world.

***

A mother's love

Is divine.

It's one of a kind.

***

<u>Adam and Eve</u>

Look down under.

A man has a penis.

A woman has a vagina.

Don't beat about the bush.

There's only ever two sexes.

***

He's very thorough.

Did not leave

A single grain of sand unturned.

Lovers' quarrel.

Only lovers

Truly understand.

***

Don't snap.

Have a nap on your lover's lap.

Let me recap.

<u>Mount Fuji</u>

Climate crisis.

Oceans keep on rising.

The summit, iceberg's tip!

***

In the rose bud

Lies a dormant rainbow.

Humanoid's love
As beautiful as a Grecian urn
Lacks the warmth of human's love and lust.

***

Bee stings.
Then buzz off.

***

I'm a seed.
All I need
Is a raindrop.

***

<u>Out in the cold</u>
A bridge for a roof, cardboard for a bed.
Dustbin for a larder. No dreams, no love, no hate.
Blank stares, hopelessness. Down in a deep dark abyss
It's heavy lifting to restore pride and self-worth.

Peonies

The old park bench
Is still sitting pretty there
Surrounded by new blooms
Where once my true love and I
Used to sit holding hands
Gazing in each other eyes
Whispering I love you.

Love is
Worth sowing.

***

Morning has broken.
The heart still in two.
Will it heal? Will it die?

***

The Blue Jay is still shy.
We've met a few times.

***

Birds sings new songs
To greet me each blessed morning.

A firefly
Landed on my palm.
A spark of joy.
Fleeting but lasting.

***

Mount Fuji.
Sakura season.
So lucky to be
Surrounded by Wisteria
Serenaded by Cherry blossoms
In full bloom erupts with joy!!

***

Fireflies.
Femmes fatales.
Have males for supper
Under their glowing light.

***

From pub to pub
Crawled and crawled till legless.
Hangover outlasted the long weekend.

Children like rivers cannot stay still.
Let boys be boys.
Girls be girls.
***

Never said a prayer
In all his life.
A thousand said
In his memory.
***

<u>No matter</u>
In joy and in happiness, in grief and in sadness
Flowers bud, bloom and grow in merry month of May.
***

Did not aim to get rich.
Out of good habits
Spent less, saved and invested the rest.
Got what I deserved.
***

Camellia falls at once
Like the head severed
By the guillotine at the Bastille.

Pollution

Affects

Reproduction.

***

Friend and foe

I cannot distinguish

Your shadow.

***

Fat cat

On a diet

Slim fit

Shadow.

***

<u>It's relative</u>

To get ahead

I competed

Against idiots.

***

Canary set free

See light of day

Chirps loudest on freedom day.

Some say the end is nigh.

They're hopeful.

They'll soon learn that misery has a long life.

Joy is short-lived.

***

The sorry state we're in

A full pink moon

A sight to behold

May cause anxiety to some.

WW3

The prospects for war are good.

We've created the perfect conditions

To succeed in Armageddon.

The soil still damp with blood of the fallen.

Greenbelt land secured for dead heroes.

Widows' war pensions well-funded.

New orphanages built, pharmacies well stocked.

Sound the bugle, bayonet in front, forward march.

Poster from a Daylily

I'll be gone for the rest of the day.

Be back tomorrow, bright and early.

I'll fall in the fall, be back even lovelier in springtime.

I need my beauty sleep, so I hibernate all winter.

Coal in mourning

Coal served its purpose.
The Industrial Revolution
Powered Empires to greatness.

Miners would not mind.
It seemed right, a fitting end.
The canary is free.

Let coal rest in peace.
Ten thousand feet underground.
A well-deserved rest.

Freezing rain.
What a pain.
Power outage.
How inconvenient for my goldfish.
***

Papal decree.
PayPal accepted
For Sunday collections.
***

The case
Of the illegal dumping
Was thrown out of court
On dubious ground.
***

With low expectations
I tend to overachieve.
Low hanging fruits first.
Not going out on a limb.

<u>Good grief!</u>

Ring the shiny copper bell.

All is well that ends well.

It's been six long years.

No cancer. Full of cheers.

Got it in the neck, the lump.

Lucky it was not in the liver.

Will it return? Will it recur?

Don't know, don't really care.

It'll not scare. No fear. I'm still here.

***

To save a life

I wrote a book.

"A Tale of Two Diseases"

Mission accomplished.

To make assurance double sure

I wrote "Cancer Recurrence Prevention"

Hoping to save yet another life.

Trial and tribulation

Go through hoops and loops.

Good at hula hoops like a sega dancer.

Avoid loan sharks, great whites and hammerheads.

Through mud, mists and fog, emerged neat and clean

Conscience as light of day, sleep without nightmares.

Friends are few, regrets fewer. Owe no one. No debtor.

Can be trusted. Don't do bad things, doesn't get noticed.

Mind my own business. Wish no one to own mine.

If there's anything else, I'll keep it for myself.

It's time for a nap.

Dark clouds. Sun shy.
Frosted leaves.
SAD season.

***

Give loyalty where it's due.
Give respect when it's deserved.
Betrayal, wish them well in hell.

***

Does it hurt
Sitting on
Piles of cash?

***

Watch out.
Pray out loud.
Mantises have hatched.

***

Actors fake feelings.
To most of us
They come naturally.

Success never final.
Failure never fatal.
Learn from them both.
There may be more of one
And less of the other.

***

<u>Eat humble pie</u>
How on earth can I not be humbled
By the nest-building skill of birds?

***

In god I trust
In me, I trust even more.

***

<u>The art of wooing</u>
It's fashionable.
Blind dates! Speed dating!
We've lost the art of wooing.
Watch Birds of paradise.
Wooing, winning, seducing
Like Don Juan.

Poles apart.

Once upon a time
I hit granite bottom. Ouch!
That was the best platform to fall on.
Like a breath of fresh air I rose to meet the stars.
***

The forget-me-not
You sent scented years ago
Is still pressed, still fresh as a Daisy.
***

Times have changed.
Things don't look the same.
Flowers in a mirror, Moon in the water
Are sad reflections of who we once were.
***

Brisk walkers tend to outlive dawdlers!
Mauritian tortoises live to be 100+.
Cheetahs die before middle age.
I walk faster than a snail
Slower than an ass on fire.

Do you still remember
Ping Pong diplomacy
Between East and West?
Could a Pickle ball diplomacy
Works the same magic
Between Dragon and Eagle?
Would the Bear find it unbearable?

***

A black hole
That's science.
An asshole
That's judgment.
A toad in the hole
That's Brit fare.

***

Winter's gone.
Roads cratered.
Filled and refilled.
Holes stayed whole.
Fit only for tadpoles.

Bud dormant.
Never made it
To the flower show.

***

<u>Danger</u>
Manger
Nager
Noyer.

***

<u>Anachronism</u>
Samurai
Wearing a Swatch
Eating samosas.

***

<u>Through the ages</u>
Young and promising.
Midlife crisis.
Old and useless.

Bird in the sky
Bird's eye view of humans.
Too polite to twit.

***

Ram is horny
Ewe is less so.

***

Lacking in
Uselessness, hopelessness?
Unhappiness, gloominess?
Tell us how to turn our lives round.

***

Stop daydreaming.
Wake up.
Do a day's work.

***

Inhale hate.
Exhale love.
Keep breathing.
Love conquers.

Drone roam the sky

I'm a kamikaze drone.

All dressed to explode.

Looking down from high up

Like a pair of eagle's eyes

I can see in the trenches

Soldiers huddled in fear.

It did not dawn on them

That I'm a friend of theirs

Flying the same blue and yellow flag.

The drone load is for the other side.

Take care. God bless.

Simple Simon

Not envious. No resentment.

Pays attention to his investment.

Cheerful in spite of troubles.

Lacking in gloominess, hopelessness.

Lacking in toxic family and friends.

Life is good. Simon kept it simple.

***

Faces are lies. Necks tell no lies.

So what's next? Love your neck.

Tie a beautiful scarf round it.

***

Who rule?

Can't rule out

I may be wrong.

Can rule in that I'm right.

***

An optimist – No.

A pessimist – No.

A possi-bilist – Yeah!

A takeover
Sonic the hedgehog
Buys
Angry birds for a song.

***

My books and looks.
I came out best in one
Second best in the other.
Can't win them all?

***

Cactus flower
On a full moon, when you bloom
I'll be dead and gone.
100 years wait is too long.

***

Sobbing faces
I empathize.
Fake smiles
I despise.

<u>It's elementary</u>
The thread goes
Where the needle goes.
Follow the thread
You'll find the needle
In the haystack.

***

<u>My kind of New Year</u>
Glass of champagne.
Pink with excitement.
Bubbling with kindness.
Overflowing with happiness.
Full of hope, love and cheers.
Annus mirabilis 2024.

An enchanted house

"La maison ou j'ai grandi n'existait plus".

On the corner of La Rampe Street and Remy Ollier Street, facing "la citadelle" Fort Adelaide and Mount Pouce, once stood proudly a "jambalac" tree, also known as Portuguese plum, bearing fruits and offering shades to all "locataires" living together in harmony and peace in a big house made of wood, filled with happy and nostalgic memories, a secure home to many faced with daily survival and an uncertain bleak future.

The tree and the old house survived cyclone Carole. We triumphed over many of life's hardships and adversities of the fifties and sixties to prosper through education, our salvation.

Today, many of us, are as old as that old house then, thriving in distant lands still remember old acquaintances, having gone through hard times, sad times and good times together.

In our golden years, we are living out our golden age.

Look at those trees.
None perfect. None imperfect.
Look at those humans.
None perfect. All imperfect.
Trees are useful and beautiful.

About The Book

On January 1, 2023, I wrote my first 3 line poem – **[Cherry blossoms/ Memories of old/ Coming to the fore]** A loose Haiku of 14 syllables. A poem a day, everyday, inspired by an article in CNN – Opinion – 17 syllables Haiku poem and the transformational effects it has on people's personal lives.. Momentum is on, I just can't stop. No brakes. I'm on a roll. By the end of 2023, a book was born– 'Bamboo Shoots", a collection of more than 400 poems of differing length, but mostly 3 – 5 lines, covering many everyday topics. Writing poems need qualities and skills that I didn't have in abundance – sit/watch/observe. **[The blue jay is still shy/ We met a few times.]** Poems on fragility of life – cherry blossoms – dazzling, swift and brief life filled with beauty. Finding inspiration under the shade of a lilac tree, looking at an empty street in winter or a wander in the local park. So much to see if only we learn to be aware of nature and human nature all around us. Writing makes your imagination fertile, liven your life, relive own life experiences on paper – surprise yourself with who you were and who you're now. Tomorrow's self can wait. Can you see beauty – **[Sun rises – is this the beginning? Sun sets – is this the end? Both are beautiful/ From beginning** to end]. We are all unique – [the sparrow does not understand the mind of a swallow] This book is inexpensive. I wrote it with audacity and without fear of judgment.

Writing poems does not make me a poet. I can fix a leaky tap, but plumber, I'm certainly not. I write for pleasure. It lessens the pressure of life, you forget to worry, it's a sort of escapism. There's joy and contentment in short poems, long in meaning, original thoughts through observation, imagination and inspiration. It's liberating. Your mind is set free to wander at will. This is a good starter book of poems. Your review would be greatly appreciated.

Manufactured by Amazon.ca
Acheson, AB

12852069R00090